uk J917.552
Gurney
MOUNT VERNON

COP 4

| | | |
|---|---|---|
| JUL 15 '69 | SHAFTER | |
| FEB 2 '81 | FRAZIER PARK | |
| DEC 1 5 '80 | TEHACHAPI | |
| | | |
| | | |
| | | |
| | | |
| | | |
| | | |
| | | |
| | | |
| | | |

## Kern County Library

1. Books may be kept until last due date on card in this pocket.

2. A fine will be charged on each book which is not returned by date due.

3. All injuries to books beyond reasonable wear and all losses shall be made good to the satisfaction of the librarian.

4. Each borrower is held responsible for all books borrowed by him and for all fines accruing on them.

DEMCO

# MOUNT VERNON

# MOUNT VERNON

by Gene and Clare Gurney

*Photographs by Harold Wise*

FRANKLIN WATTS, INC.
575 Lexington Ave., New York, N.Y. 10022

# Contents

A MEMORIAL TO OUR FIRST PRESIDENT 1

THE MANSION HOUSE FARM 2

THE WASHINGTONS AND MOUNT VERNON 3

MOUNT VERNON BECOMES A MEMORIAL 8

THE MOUNT VERNON MANSION HOUSE 9

THE FIRST FLOOR 11

THE SECOND FLOOR 26

THE OUTBUILDINGS 33

THE GROUNDS 49

THE MUSEUM 52

WASHINGTON'S TOMB 55

THE TRADITIONAL SALUTE 58

WASHINGTON'S GRIST MILL 58

WOODLAWN PLANTATION 61

POHICK CHURCH 63

A MOUNT VERNON CHRONOLOGY 65

GENERAL INFORMATION 68

INDEX 69

*A circular driveway leads to Mount Vernon's west front. Washington's sundial stands in the middle of the courtyard.*

## A Memorial to Our First President

MOUNT VERNON, the stately mansion on the Potomac River that was George Washington's home for many years, now serves as a memorial to our first President. Located in the beautiful Virginia countryside about sixteen miles from Washington, D. C., Mount Vernon is visited by millions of people each year. These people find that a trip to Mount Vernon provides not only an authentic picture of how George Washington lived, but also gives an understanding of an important period of American history.

The home of the first President of the United States has been carefully restored by the Mount Vernon Ladies' Association of the Union, a nonprofit organization which holds it in trust as a national shrine. When the Association acquired Mount Vernon in 1858, most of George and Martha Washington's possessions had been scattered about among their descendants. There were numerous descriptions and records of what had been at Mount Vernon, however, and the Association set about recovering as many of the articles as possible. In the meantime, the house itself and the adjacent buildings were restored as research revealed their original appearance. Modern heating, lighting, and fire protection systems have been added, but for the most part they are concealed from public view.

The grounds surrounding the mansion have also been restored, so that once again they look as they did when George and Martha Washington lived at Mount Vernon. Also, many of the records on which the Association based its restoration of the house and grounds are now on display at Mount Vernon, along with other items that belonged to the Washington family.

1

## The Mansion House Farm

GEORGE WASHINGTON loved the outdoors. In addition to his fame as a soldier and a statesman, the first President won wide recognition as one of the leading agriculturists of his day. His Mount Vernon estate was large — over 8,000 acres divided into five separate farms. Each farm had its own manager, workers, equipment, and animals.

Washington called the 500-acre farm on which his own house was located "Mansion House Farm." It is the present-day Mount Vernon. At Mansion House Farm, Washington did very little real farming. He used some of it for testing new crops and farming methods. Areas closer to the house were devoted to flower and vegetable gardens, fruit trees and vineyards. But Washington developed much of his Mansion House Farm as a park to serve as a beautiful setting for his house, and that is how it is preserved today.

*George Washington made this drawing of Mount Vernon when he was fourteen years old. Note the small house in the upper left-hand corner. When the drawing was made the house had not yet been enlarged to its later size.*

## The Washingtons and Mount Vernon

THE FIRST WASHINGTON to own the property that later became Mount Vernon was John. He was George Washington's great-grandfather and he migrated to Virginia from England in the year 1657. In 1674, John and another colonist, Nicholas Spencer, acquired 5,000 acres of rich farmland on the Virginia side of the Potomac River. The two families owned the land together until 1690. Then, because both John and Nicholas had died, the property was divided among their children.

John Washington's share went to his son Lawrence, and then to Lawrence's daughter Mildred. In 1726, Mildred Washington Gregory sold the property, which had been named Little Hunting Creek Plantation, to her brother Augustine. Augustine was George Washington's father.

Augustine Washington and his family lived on the Virginia estate now called Wakefield, where George was born in the year 1732. When he was three, the family moved to Little Hunting Creek Plantation, but their stay there was a short one. In 1739, the house that Augustine built at Little Hunting Creek Plantation may have burned down. Few records remain to tell us what actually happened. At any rate, Augustine moved his family to another estate that he owned near Fredericksburg, Virginia. The following year he gave Little Hunting Creek Plantation to his eldest son, Lawrence.

It was Lawrence who named the estate Mount Vernon, after Admiral Edward Vernon, on whose ship Lawrence had served in the Caribbean. After Lawrence married in 1743, he lived at Mount Vernon. Following the death of Augustine that same year, the orphaned George Washington spent much of his time at his brother's house.

When Lawrence died, Mount Vernon became the property of

3

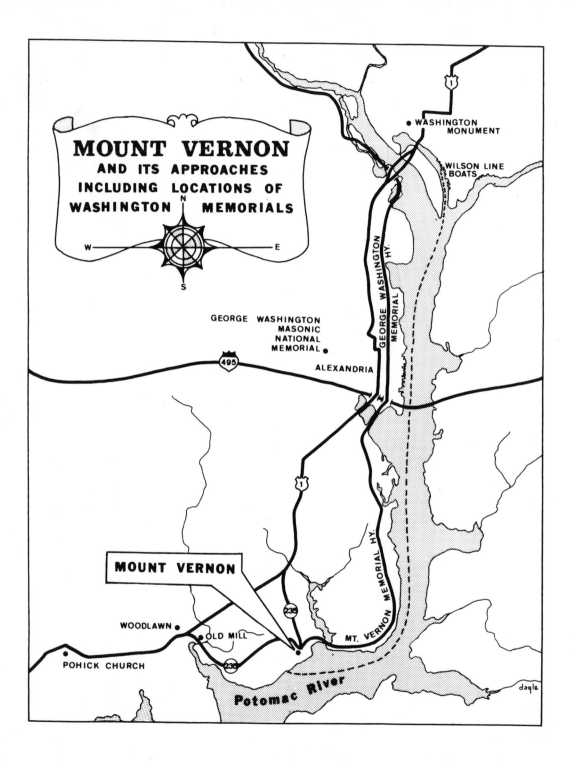

MOUNT VERNON
AND ITS APPROACHES
INCLUDING LOCATIONS OF
WASHINGTON MEMORIALS

N
W — E
S

WASHINGTON MONUMENT

WILSON LINE BOATS

GEORGE WASHINGTON MEMORIAL HY.

GEORGE WASHINGTON MASONIC NATIONAL MEMORIAL

495

ALEXANDRIA

1

MOUNT VERNON

235

MT. VERNON MEMORIAL HY.

WOODLAWN

OLD MILL

235

POHICK CHURCH

Potomac River

dagle

*George Washington.*

his daughter Sarah, but Sarah outlived her father only briefly. In 1754, George purchased the life interest held by Sarah's mother, and became the owner of the estate.

Although he was still in his early twenties, George had already worked for several years as a surveyor. He now turned enthusiastically to farming his own estate, which he considered to be one of the best in the entire Virginia colony. He also began to enlarge his house, which then consisted of only the central portion of the present mansion. The one-and-a-half-story dwelling had a hall flanked by four small rooms on the first floor and four rooms on the floor above.

However, Washington's ambitious plans for improving Mount Vernon were delayed somewhat by his military service during the French and Indian War. That conflict broke out in 1754, over rival British and French claims to North America. The thirteen colonies sided, of course, with their mother country, Great Britain. Washington served as an aide to General Braddock, the commander of the British forces and, after Braddock's death, as commander of the Virginia Militia. While he was away, his young brother John managed Mount Vernon, and a friend and neighbor, William Fairfax, supervised the remodeling of the house.

George returned home to Virginia in 1758. On January 6, 1759, he married Martha Dandridge Custis, a widow with two children and a considerable fortune.

*Martha Washington.*

For the next several years, Washington devoted himself to caring for his property. He had enlarged Mount Vernon by purchasing the adjoining land owned by the Spencers, but in spite of its increased size, Washington managed to supervise closely the many activities of his estate. He also continued with improvements on the house. His plans called for the addition of rooms at both ends of the central portion, as well as several changes in the surrounding grounds.

Washington's plans for Mount Vernon were still far from completed when the growing tension between Great Britain and her American colonies erupted into open warfare. On June 15, 1775, the Continental Congress chose Washington to lead the military forces of the colonies in their struggle for independence from Great Britain. He took command of the Continental Army at Boston on July 3. During the next eight years the General visited Mount Vernon only once. In his absence, his cousin Lund Washington managed the five farms and continued with the improvements on the estate.

The Revolutionary War ended in 1783. Washington resigned his commission and hurried back to his beloved Mount Vernon. His only ambition now was to become the "first farmer in the country." But Washington was held in such high esteem by his countrymen that he was unanimously elected the first President of the United States in 1789. Once more he left Mount Vernon, this time for New York, where his inauguration took place on April 30, 1789.

During his two terms as President, Washington was able to visit Mount Vernon only occasionally. From New York and Philadelphia (Washington, D. C. did not become the capital until 1800), he kept in close touch with affairs at Mount Vernon. His manager sent him weekly reports, and Washington, in turn, sent detailed directions for work that he wanted done.

Although he was offered a third term as President, Washington refused it and returned to Mount Vernon in 1797. During the next two and a half years he devoted himself entirely to his family and his estate.

George Washington died at Mount Vernon on December 14, 1799, and was buried in the family tomb overlooking the Potomac River. Martha Washington died in 1802 and was buried beside him.

Mount Vernon then became the property of Washington's nephew, Bushrod Washington, who was an Associate Justice of the Supreme Court. Because of his judicial duties, the new owner was able to spend but little time at Mount Vernon. When he died, he willed the estate to a nephew, John Augustine Washington, Sr.,

The last private owner of Mount Vernon, John Augustine Washington, Jr., received it as a wedding gift in 1850.

## Mount Vernon Becomes a Memorial

By 1850, MOUNT VERNON was no longer productive as a farm, but the home of the first President of the United States had become a popular tourist attraction. Concerned for its protection and preservation, John Augustine Washington, Jr., offered it first to the state of Virginia and then to the federal government. Neither was interested in acquiring the property.

A group of public-spirited women, under the leadership of Miss Ann Pamela Cunningham, then organized the Mount Vernon Ladies' Association of the Union, and inaugurated a campaign to raise enough money to buy the estate. In 1858, they were able to purchase the house and 200 acres of land surrounding it. They then began to restore the house and grounds as a memorial to George Washington. Subsequent purchases increased the Association's holdings to almost 500 acres, so that the Mount Vernon of today corresponds closely to Washington's Mansion House Farm.

8

*Miss Ann Pamela Cunningham. This portrait of the founder of the Mount Vernon Ladies' Association hangs in the Mount Vernon Museum. She directed the activities of the Association until 1874.*

## The Mount Vernon Mansion House

WASHINGTON'S HOUSE at Mount Vernon is Georgian in style — that is, its style of architecture was popular when George I, George II, and George III were kings of England. Many houses like it were built in England and America during the eighteenth century. Georgian architecture has been described as "formal and elegant." Visitors to Mount Vernon will agree that it is also beautiful.

Mount Vernon's most striking feature, the eight-columned piazza (a veranda or porch) that runs across the east front of the house, is not typical of Georgian architecture. Washington probably de-

*Mount Vernon today.*

signed it himself, but the piazza was erected in 1777 while he was away from Mount Vernon fighting the British. While the Revolutionary War lasted, suitable paving stones for the floor could not be obtained. Finally, in 1786, a shipment of stone arrived from England and the floor was finished. The white paving stones now on the piazza floor came from the same quarry that furnished the original ones. On warm days in the summer, the Washingtons and their friends sat on the piazza, and from it enjoyed a magnificent view of the Potomac River.

## The First Floor

FROM GEORGE WASHINGTON's famous piazza, double doors lead to the broad central hall that runs through the house from front to rear. On either side of the hall, which the Washingtons called "the passage," are the principal rooms of the first floor. The hall itself contains many interesting articles that belonged to the first President.

## Floor Plans of the Mansion

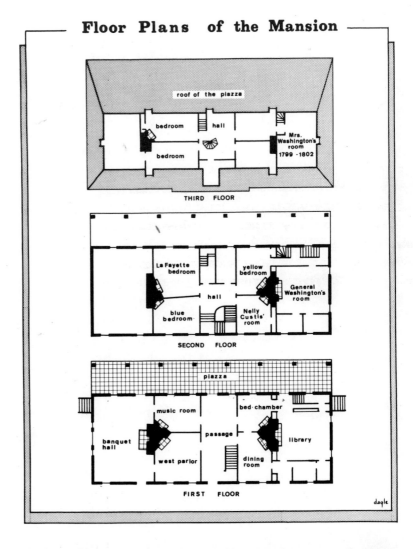

On one wall hangs a large key. Once it opened the main entrance to the Bastille, the famous prison in Paris, France. When the prison was destroyed during the French Revolution, the Marquis de Lafayette, the French general who fought for the colonies during the Revolutionary War, sent the key to his old commander, George Washington. A model of the Bastille, made from the original stone, stands on a small table.

Above the double doors leading from the piazza are two plaster lions. They have been identified as the "two lyons" ordered from England and received at Mount Vernon in 1760. Several other items now in the hall were there when the Washingtons lived at Mount Vernon. They include the barometer, which George Washington consulted regularly; the tables with marble tops; the clock on the landing; the lantern; and some of the prints hanging on the walls.

The large banquet hall on the north side of the mansion was planned before the Revolutionary War and constructed while Washington was serving as commander of the Continental Army. It is an example of the many major changes made at Mount Vernon during Washington's lifetime, even though he was often away from home. During the building of the banquet hall, he wrote many letters about it to his estate manager, Lund Washington. One letter, written in 1776, contains these directions: "The chimney of the new room shall be exactly in the middle of it — the doors and everything else to be exactly answerable and uniform — in short, I would have the whole executed in a masterly manner."

The handsome room has been restored to look as it did in Washington's time. Its colorful furnishings include mahogany chairs with yellow damask seats, and green satin drapes hanging at the windows. One of the windows is an impressive Palladian window that reaches almost to the ceiling. Washington preferred plain wallpaper in a green or blue color. A scrap of the original wall covering led to the choice of the present green wallpaper.

*Left: George Washington climbed these stairs many, many times. The lantern hanging from the stairs was given to Lawrence Washington by Admiral Edward Vernon, for whom Mount Vernon was named. The table at the right holds George Washington's model of the Bastille. Right: Lawrence Washington placed this clock on the stair landing and it remained there during the years George Washington was master of Mount Vernon. The clock still runs.*

*George Washington entertained his many friends in Mount Vernon's banquet hall.
He called it "the new room."*

The elaborately carved marble mantel came from England as a
present from an admirer, Samuel Vaughan. Ocean pirates are said
to have intercepted the ship carrying the mantel and other valuable cargo to the United States. When the pirates discovered that
the mantel was destined for George Washington, the famous American general, they feared for their lives and sent that part of their
loot on to Mount Vernon.

When Washington received the mantel in 1785, he wrote to
Vaughan: "The chimney-piece is arrived and, by the number of
cases (ten), too elegant and costly by far. I fear for my own room
and republican style of living."

Samuel Vaughan also gave Washington the vases now displayed on the mantel.

Washington personally supervised the work on the stucco ceiling of the banquet hall, which is a story-and-a-half high. Much to his dismay, the ceiling later cracked.

The west parlor, a paneled room adjoining the banquet hall, is believed to date from George Washington's first enlargement of the house, which took place just before his marriage. It has the decorated ceiling, elaborate doorframes, and paneled walls that were fashionable in colonial Virginia. High above the fireplace in this room is the carved and painted Washington coat of arms. Below the coat of arms hangs the "neat landskip" that Washington ordered from his agent in England. It is, of course, a landscape.

*"Too elegant and costly by far" was the way Washington described the banquet hall mantel, a gift from an English friend.*

The west parlor contains many family portraits. The companion pastels of George and Martha Washington, by James Sharples, hang there, as does a portrait of Martha Washington's niece Fanny Bassett, by Robert Edge Pine, and a portrait of George Washington as the Commander in Chief of the Continental Army, painted by Charles Wilson Peale during the Revolutionary War. There is also a portrait of George Washington Lafayette, the son of the Marquis de Lafayette. General Lafayette became a good friend of George Washington and his family, and visited Mount Vernon after the war.

A game table that belonged to Washington now stands in the west parlor. On it are playing cards, and game chips in the shape of fish. A silver tea tray is set up ready for serving.

The Washington coat of arms appears for a second time in the west parlor at the top of the mirror that hangs between the room's

*Mount Vernon's west parlor was completed just before George Washington's marriage.*

The Washington coat
of arms. George Wash-
ington used the emblem,
or a variation of it, to
mark many of his be-
longings.

Washington and his
friends played cards at
this table.

two windows. A variant of the coat of arms was cast into the iron
fireback of the fireplace opening. The fireplace emblem has *GW*
instead of mullets and bars in the shield.

Mount Vernon had another parlor which the Washingtons referred to as the little parlor, or the music room, or the common
parlor. In this room they gathered with their guests for dancing,
singing, and listening to good music. By his own admission, George
Washington could not carry a tune or play an instrument, but he
liked to dance and he was an impressive figure on the dance floor.

The little parlor contains the harpsichord that Washington imported from London in 1793 for his adopted daughter Nelly
Custis, who had already learned to play the spinet and the piano-
forte. In those days, a music master rode from house to house giving
lessons to the young people.

17

*Left: The ebony flute with silver keys lying on the table was once thought to have been Washington's, but it probably belonged to his adopted son, George Washington Parke Custis. In 1789 Washington wrote: "I can neither sing one of the songs, nor raise a single note on any instrument." Right: The urn-shaped silver lamp on the table behind the flute shows how Mount Vernon was lighted in Washington's day. The lamp burned oil. Candles were also used at Mount Vernon.*

When Nelly married and left Mount Vernon, she took the harpsichord with her to the new home which she and her husband, Lawrence Lewis, built at Woodlawn Plantation — the estate given to them by George Washington. Many years later, during the restoration of Mount Vernon, the harpsichord was returned to its old place in the little parlor, along with some of Nelly's music. A book of her music is now displayed on the harpsichord.

Like all the rooms at Mount Vernon, the little parlor contains many handsome pictures. Some of them are the same pictures that hung there in Washington's time, while others are carefully done copies. One of the original works depicts a sea engagement between the *Bonhomme Richard*, commanded by John Paul Jones, the naval hero of the Revolutionary War, and the British ship *Serapis*.

Martha Washington once made cushions for the chairs in the little parlor. They were copied for the chairs now in the room.

*One of Nelly Custis' music books.*

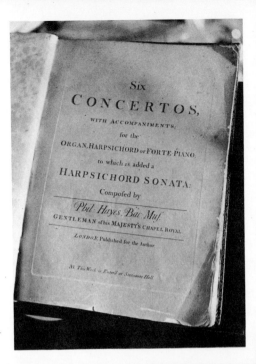

*A view of the little parlor and Nelly Custis' harpsichord.*

When they were not entertaining large numbers of guests, the Washingtons ate their meals in a family dining room that opened off the central hall. Today it contains many articles that they used: two small tables, china, silver, crystal candelabra, a punch bowl, and a tea caddy. Some of the Chippendale ladder-back chairs are original, but Washington's handsome dining table has never been located. The table now in the room is from another colonial Virginia home. Washington used the mirrored plateau on the table while he was President, and then brought it back to Mount Vernon.

The dining room sideboard, a beautiful piece of furniture, was returned to Mount Vernon by one of Martha Washington's descendants.

*A view of the family dining room showing the mirrored plateau that Washington brought back to Mount Vernon when he retired from the Presidency.*

*Washington was proud of his dining room ceiling of molded plaster decorated with gilt.*

When Nelly and George Washington Parke Custis, Martha's grandchildren, came to live at Mount Vernon after the death of their father in 1781, they were young enough to use the high chair now in the dining room.

In 1775, Washington hired two master craftsmen to decorate the dining room ceiling and mantel. He was away from Mount Vernon at the time, and Lund Washington wrote to tell him that the room was almost finished and "very pretty."

Like all Virginia landowners, Washington entertained many overnight guests, and their number increased as he became more famous. The downstairs bedroom at Mount Vernon was so often occupied by a guest that Washington referred to his house as a "well-resorted tavern."

Most large colonial homes had a huge bedroom on the first floor. At Mount Vernon it contained an ample four-poster bed. The bed and the windows were draped in bright matching chintz. The windows of this room, like many others at Mount Vernon, were equipped with Venetian blinds. The blinds there today are not the original ones, but they are similar to what Washington had in mind in 1775, when he ordered a blind "such as draws and closes and expands." He thriftily ordered just one in order that, as he explained, "others may be made by it at home."

In the large library, or study, finished in 1775, Washington kept his many books on history, farming, military affairs, geography, political science, and religion, and his personal papers. Like the matching banquet hall at the other end of the house, the library

*The library, or study, was Washington's favorite room.*

became an important feature of the enlarged mansion. It served as Washington's office where he made daily entries in his diary, posted accounts, and looked over reports from his overseers. After the Revolutionary War, he spent many hours in the library writing letters to other leaders of the young republic on the problems of the difficult postwar years.

The room now contains a desk that Washington used — a large one with a glass-doored bookcase above it. After his death, both it and the round, cushioned chair were given to Dr. James Craik, his physician. Many years later the desk and chair were returned to Mount Vernon. A terrestrial globe, made in London to Washington's order, is also on display in the library. Other authentic Washington items in the room include a riding crop, a

*Washington bought this desk when he returned to Mount Vernon after serving as the first President of the United States.*

gold-headed walking stick, a large gun for shooting ducks, and the ancient iron chest in which Washington kept important papers.

Washington owned hundreds of books; a list made after his death contained eight hundred and eighty-four titles. They were all bequeathed to his principal heir, Bushrod Washington, who in turn left them to two nephews. Over the years the books were further dispersed by sale and gift, until what would have been a priceless collection was thoroughly scattered about the country. The Mount Vernon Ladies' Association has been able to acquire some of the original volumes and bring them back to Mount Vernon. The other books on display are duplicates of the titles that once were in Washington's library.

*A pair of the first President's reading glasses can be seen in the library.*

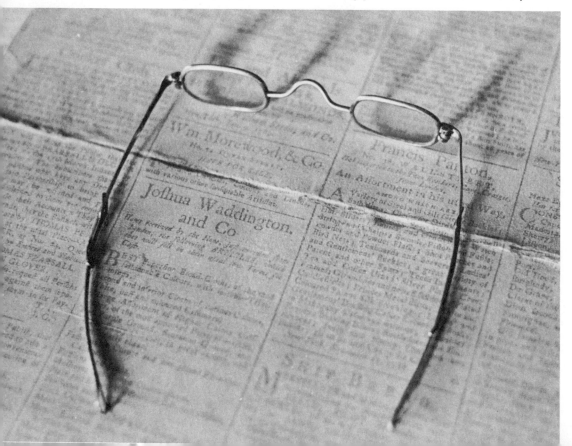

*In the pantry, Frank the butler kept china and serving utensils in neat rows.*

Mount Vernon, like all large eighteenth-century houses, had a small room near the dining room called a pantry. Food prepared in the kitchen was served from the pantry, and its shelves held the tableware in daily use. The best china was stored in a second-floor closet or in the basement. A butler named Frank presided over the pantry in George Washington's day.

Mrs. Washington's "everyday" dishes were Canton china in a blue and white pattern, but few pieces have survived. The dishes now on display in the pantry are from a similar set that President and Mrs. Washington gave to a friend in 1797. The serving utensils used at Mount Vernon were mostly of copper or pewter.

The large wine chest in a corner of the pantry was ordered from England in 1759. The description on the invoice reads: "A neat mahogany Square Case with 16 Gall'n Bottles in ditto with ground

25

stoppers, Brass lifting handles and brass Casters." When the chest arrived from England, Washington felt that he had been over-charged and he wrote a sharp complaint to his London agent: "Surely here must be as great a mistake, or as great an Imposition as ever offered by a Tradesman."

The small table now in the pantry is the one on which George and Martha Washington ate their wedding breakfast after their marriage on January 6, 1759, at Mrs. Washington's "White House" in New Kent Country, in eastern Virginia.

## The Second Floor

MOUNT VERNON'S SECOND FLOOR contains six bedrooms. The largest of these rooms, at the south end of the house above the library, was the Washingtons' sleeping quarters. The room's location, and the fact that it had a separate stairway to the floor below, gave the master and mistress some privacy when the house had its usual quota of guests.

The large four-poster in that room is the one in which Washington died on December 14, 1799. Busy as usual with improvements that he wanted to make at Mount Vernon, Washington had spent part of December 13, a cold, snowy day, on the riverbank where he planned to build a gravel walk. He became ill that night with a severe sore throat and his condition grew worse the next day. His physician, Dr. James Craik, was summoned in the morning. A few hours later, two more physicians were called in, but the distinguished patient grew steadily weaker. He died that evening.

The bed in which the first President died was returned to Mount Vernon in 1908, by the descendants of George Washington Parke Custis. Custis, a grandson of Martha Washington, obtained the bed after her death in 1802. During the intervening years, the bed, an unusually wide one, had been carefully preserved by the Custis family.

*George Washington's bedroom at Mount Vernon. This is the room in which he died on December 14, 1799.*

At the foot of Washington's bed is a trunk with his name on a brass plate. Washington bought the trunk in 1776, and used it to store his personal belongings in the military quarters which he occupied during the Revolutionary War. Washington's shaving and dressing table is also on display. It has a marble top and a mirrored lid. The Washingtons bought the table and the lady's writing desk that stands nearby from the first French minister to the United States.

Martha Washington placed a portrait of her granddaughter, Martha Parke Custis, over the desk, and it hangs there today. Above the handsome fireplace is a companion portrait of Martha's youngest granddaughter, Nelly Parke Custis. Both portraits were painted at Mount Vernon by Robert Edge Pine in 1785.

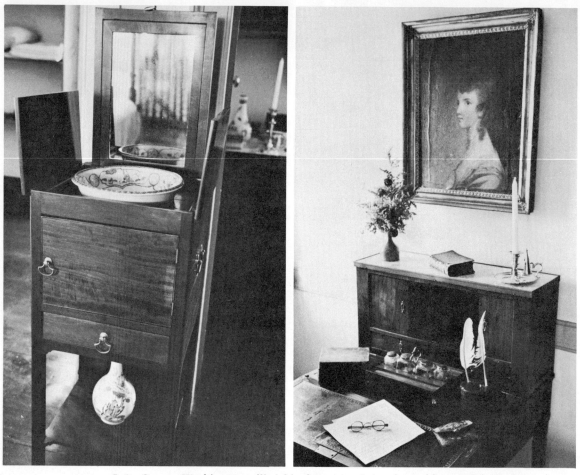

*Left: George Washington willed his shaving and dressing table to a friend. It was later returned to Mount Vernon. Right: A picture of her granddaughter and name-sake Martha Custis hung over Martha Washington's bedroom writing desk.*

Mount Vernon's Blue Bedroom received its name from its bright blue woodwork. It contains the trunk that Martha Washington used when she traveled north during the years of the Revolutionary War to spend the winter with General Washington at the head-quarters of the American Army. Fastened to the trunk lid is a letter in which one of Martha's grandchildren described the annual packing and unpacking as her grandmother prepared to leave Mount Vernon in the fall and returned home again in the spring.

*The Blue Bedroom and the trunk Martha Washington used when she visited her husband during the Revolutionary War years.*

*The Marquis de Lafayette, who called George Washington his "adopted father," slept in this room when he visited Mount Vernon.*

Adjoining the Blue Bedroom is the Lafayette Room, named for General Lafayette who slept there when he visited Mount Vernon. A very small room near the stairs was once the bedroom of George Washington Parke Custis. His sister Nelly occupied what is now called the Nelly Custis Room. It contains the white canopied crib used by Nelly's baby daughter, who was born at Mount Vernon shortly before Washington died.

*The Nelly Custis Room.*

*The Yellow Bedroom was named for the color of its wallpaper.*

Before the south addition to the house was completed, George and Martha Washington used the room called the Yellow Bedroom, next to the Nelly Custis Room. Its windows overlooked the Potomac River.

On the landing of the narrow stairway leading from the second to the third floor are the leather fire buckets that could be found in every home like Mount Vernon. Because there were no fire departments with pumpers and fire fighters in the country, the residents of each house had to be prepared to put out their own fires.

*On August 21, 1792, Nelly Custis scratched "Elisa Custis" and the date on one of the windows in the Yellow Bedroom. The writing is still visible.*

Mount Vernon's third floor, not regularly open to the public, has seven rooms. Three are bedrooms, one with a fireplace. Three others are storage rooms, and one is a storage closet. As was customary at the time, when George Washington died Martha closed up their second-floor bedroom. She moved to a small room above it on the third floor, which she used until her own death in 1802.

*George Washington bought Mount Vernon's leather fire buckets when he was living in Philadelphia during his second term as President.*

*After her husband's death, Martha Washington slept in this small, unheated room on the third floor.*

*The arched colonnade between the kitchen and the Mansion House.*

## The Outbuildings

LIKE ALL LARGE RESIDENCES of its day, the main house at Mount Vernon was supplemented by numerous outbuildings where servants lived and carried on the work of the estate. Probably the most important of these outbuildings was the kitchen which, at Mount Vernon, was connected to the house by a curved colonnade. The Washingtons' kitchen staff usually consisted of two cooks and two waiters who worked under the supervision of a steward or a housekeeper.

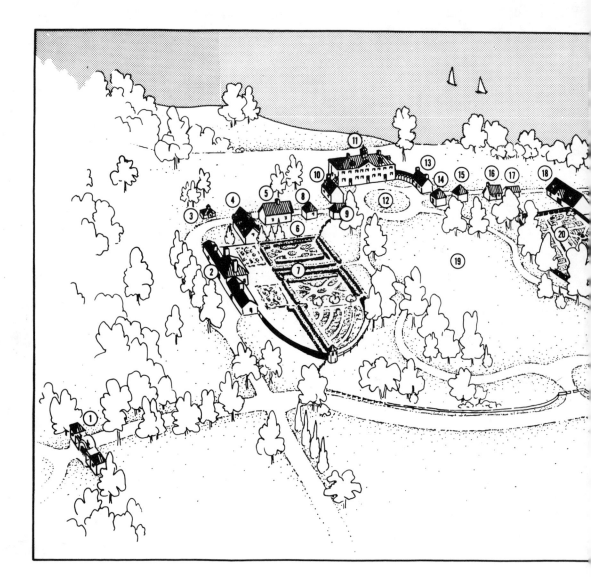

1 Entrance
2 Greenhouse and Quarters
3 Icehouse
4 Museum
5 Spinning House
6 Botanical Garden
7 Flower Garden

8 Storehouse
9 Gardener's House
10 Office
11 Mansion
12 Courtyard
13 Kitchen
14 Storehouse and Butler's Quarters

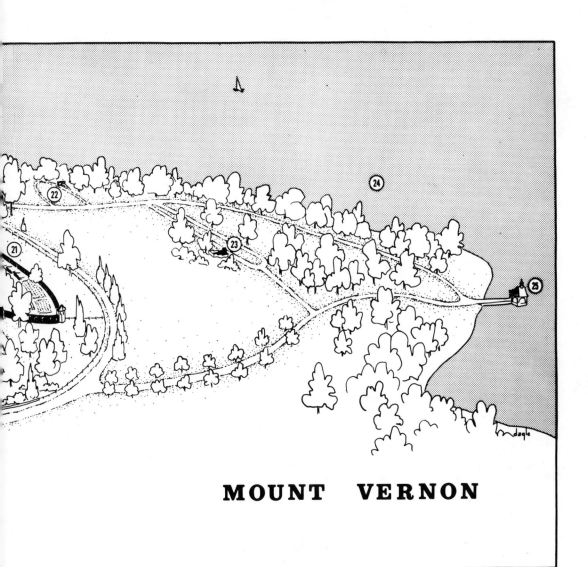

# MOUNT VERNON

15 Smokehouse
16 Washhouse
17 Coachhouse
18 Stable
19 Bowling Green
20 Vegetable Garden
21 Paddock

22 Old Washington Family Tomb
23 Washington's Tomb
24 Potomac River
25 Wharf

*The kitchen at Mount Vernon.*

The Mount Vernon cooks prepared large quantities of food every day because, in addition to the several people living in the house, there were numerous guests to cook for. Breakfast was served at 7 A.M., dinner at 3 P.M., tea at 6 P.M., and supper at 9 P.M. For breakfast, a guest reported having both cold and boiled meat and a choice of tea or coffee. Dinner was a hearty meal. One Mount Vernon visitor was offered roast pig, boiled leg of lamb, roast fowl, beef, peas, lettuce, cucumbers, and artichokes, with puddings and tarts for dessert. Wine, beer, and cider were available. George Washington himself preferred a fine Madeira wine.

*Food for the Washingtons and their guests was prepared at the kitchen fireplace.*

*Bread was baked in an oven built into the wall next to the fireplace.*

The kitchen, with its huge fireplace for cooking, remained relatively unchanged over the years, but few of the original kitchen utensils have survived. The utensils now in the kitchen were in use in Washington's time, but many of them are from other houses. A large iron mortar for grinding corn, some of the pewter plates with hot-water compartments for keeping food warm, an iron-stand, a trivit, and a bell-metal skillet have been identified as part of the kitchen's original equipment.

The building next to the kitchen in the south service lane was known as the butler's house, but it seems also to have been used by the storekeeper who issued tools and materials to the men and

*Left: Like all Mount Vernon rooms, the Lafayette Room was heated by a fireplace. The long-handled object on the right was filled with live coals and placed in the bed to warm it in winter. Right: George Washington Parke Custis slept in this room when he lived at Mount Vernon as a boy.*

*Left: Candles were made in a small room off the kitchen. Right: Semiperishable foods were kept in a pantry in the kitchen building that was specially constructed to maintain a cool temperature.*

39

*This mortar, used for crushing corn and other grains, was in the kitchen when Washington lived at Mount Vernon.*

women working at Mount Vernon. The shoemaker got his leather there, the carpenter his nails, and so on through a long list of activities. The estate was very nearly self-sufficient and almost everything needed to keep it running was produced and stored on the premises.

Three small buildings farther along the south service lane were used as a smokehouse, a washhouse, and a coach house. They have been restored and are open to the public. The two-wheeled riding chair now in the coach house belonged to Washington's friend, Lord Thomas Fairfax.

*The living quarters in the butler's house.*

The storehouse in the front part of the butler's house has been stocked with the many tools and other items it must have held when George Washington lived at Mount Vernon.

Records show that in January, 1776, 132 hogs were butchered at Mount Vernon. Most of the meat would have been cured in the smokehouse.

*The washhouse has been re-equipped with items similar to those that inventory records indicate were in it at the time of Washington's death.*

The last building on the south service lane is a large brick stable, built in 1782 to replace a frame stable destroyed by fire. The stable was used primarily to house Washington's horses and those of his guests. Among its residents were Washington's Arabian stallion Magnolia, who won fame as a racehorse, and Nelson, who lived to a ripe old age after serving as Washington's mount throughout the Revolutionary War. Nelson was named for his donor, General Thomas Nelson. During the war, Washington occasionally rode another horse, named Blueskin, but Blueskin never got used to the sound of gunfire.

*The Mount Vernon coach house and Lord Fairfax's two-wheeled riding chair.*

When he was at Mount Vernon, Washington rode through some part of his property each day to supervise the operation of his farms. He wrote to a friend: "This [breakfast] over, I mount my horse and ride round my farms, which employs me until it is time to dress for dinner." During the hunting season he often took his hounds with him.

*Stalls for horses line both sides of the stable. Washington owned both saddle and carriage horses.*

Washington's carriage horses pulled a series of fashionable vehicles during his lifetime, but none has ever been located. The coach that now stands in the coach compartment of the stable was built by the same Philadelphia coachmaker who made coaches for the first President. Washington is thought to have ridden in this one and he owned one that was identical except for the decoration.

In the north service lane, the building closest to the house was used for a variety of purposes. At different times it served as a servants' hall, guesthouse, and a manager's residence and office. The Mount Vernon Ladies' Association now uses it as an administrative office.

*Washington rode in this coach when he was President and he owned one similar to it. It is on display in the coach compartment of the stable.*

*Numerous pieces of farm equipment similar to those used at Mount Vernon in Washington's day are on display outside the stable.*

*A view of the north service lane.*

Three buildings farther down the north service lane were used as a gardener's house, a storehouse, and a spinning house. The gardener's house was also used by the shoemaker and the tailor, both of whom were employed full-time at Mount Vernon to take care of the needs of the many people living on the estate. Records indicate that the shoemaker could turn out as many as two hundred and seventeen pairs of shoes a year, in addition to repairing one hundred and ninety-one pairs. All these shoes were worn by the residents of the estate who, in 1786, numbered ninety at the Mansion House Farm. One hundred and fifty more, mostly field hands, lived on the other four farms.

Cloth for the garments they wore came from the spinning house where twelve workers spun, knit, and wove the wool, flax, and cotton fibers that were grown on Washington's farms. In 1768, for example, the spinning house produced more than 800 yards of linen, 365 yards of woolen cloth, and 150 yards of a combination of wool and linen called linsey-woolsey. The spinning wheels, reels, and other equipment now in the spinning house are typical of the implements used to make cloth in Washington's day.

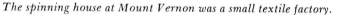

*The spinning house at Mount Vernon was a small textile factory.*

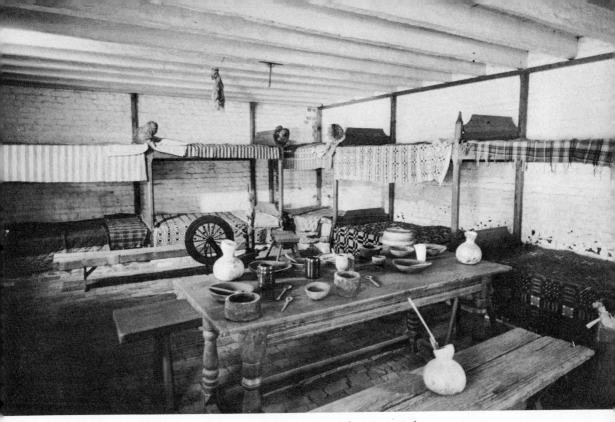

*Each room in the servants' quarters housed several people. Most of the servants at Mount Vernon were Negro slaves. On February 18, 1786, Washington counted 41 adult Negroes and 26 children at his Mansion House Farm. He also employed white indentured servants who worked for him in exchange for their passage from Europe and other benefits agreed to in a contract, or indenture.*

Washington built his greenhouse, a two-story building flanked by servants' quarters, in 1785. In the greenhouse, which faced his flower garden, he successfully grew plants from many countries. Both the greenhouse and the servants' quarters burned down in 1835. They were later rebuilt on the same site and the present structures very closely resemble the greenhouse and quarters of 1785.

Fire was an ever-present danger during Mount Vernon's early days, and several buildings, in addition to the greenhouse and servants' quarters, burned down. Today, the Mount Vernon Ladies'

47

Association takes numerous precautions to safeguard the house and the surrounding structures. Mount Vernon has its own fire truck. There is plenty of water available and automatic fire detectors have been installed. As a further precaution, the estate's central heating plant is located some 400 feet from the mansion house.

No one is permitted in the mansion house after dark. Powerful searchlights play over Mount Vernon at night to discourage those who might try to climb over the estate's walls. Guards, accompanied by watchdogs, make regular rounds, and electric eyes give added protection against intruders.

*George Washington Parke Custis and his sister Nelly received part of their education in this "schoolhouse" located at the edge of the flower garden.*

*The entrance to Mount Vernon. It is about one mile east of the gate that George Washington used.*

## The Grounds

ALTHOUGH GEORGE WASHINGTON never visited England, the lawns and gardens at Mount Vernon closely resembled those of an English country house. There were areas of meadows, woods, parks, vineyards, and gardens for flowers and vegetables.

At Mount Vernon, the formal gardens and lawns were separated from the farm fields on three sides by sunken brick walls with deep ditches on the outside called "ha-has." A gardener took care of the planted areas within the walls, but Washington closely supervised his work. He also planned — and when he was home, supervised — the improvements that were always under way somewhere on the grounds.

49

In 1785, Washington began the development of the bowling green, the large grassy area on the west side of the house. The game of bowls, or lawn bowling, was very popular in early America. It required a level lawn, or green, on which the players tried to roll wooden bowls as close as possible to a stationary ball called a jack. Washington's bowling green was enclosed by a serpentine drive leading to the carriage entrance to the mansion house. In his diary, Washington mentions the grading of the lawn area and the planting of the trees and shrubs that border it. Some of the trees are still standing.

Washington's flower garden, on one side of the bowling green, was a large one, but there is no record of the many kinds of flowers that must have grown there. It is known that he raised fruit trees, ornamental trees and shrubs, many of them imported varieties. Tropical plants were grown in large wooden boxes so that they could be moved into the greenhouse during the winter.

The kitchen, or vegetable, garden occupied the other side of the bowling green. The Washingtons raised most of the food that they and their guests ate. Consequently, a wide variety of vegetables, fruits, berries, and herbs grew in the kitchen garden. The garden has been restored, and the various items that grew there in Washington's time are growing there today. The greenhouse and an outdoor botanical garden used for experimental planting contain the same kinds of plants that they did when Washington lived at Mount Vernon. The flower garden has been replanted with the flowers found in most Virginia gardens of the period. The carefully preserved boxwood hedges, however, date from Washington's day.

The bowling green, the gardens, and the outbuildings were all located on the west side of the mansion house. It was from the west that travelers approached Mount Vernon. They rode through the west lodge gate, almost a mile west of the present entrance, and

The box hedges in the flower garden are the same ones that Washington planted there.

During the summer, excursion boats from the city of Washington dock regularly at the Mount Vernon wharf.

up the serpentine drive that ran on both sides of the bowling green and circled the courtyard at the carriage entrance to the house.

On the east side of the mansion, Washington's carefully planned landscaping made the most of the majestic Potomac view. The park-like expanse of lawn sloping down to the riverbank was dotted with trees that were spaced to permit a view of the water and the low, wooded hills of Maryland on the opposite shore.

In describing Mount Vernon to a friend, Washington wrote: "No estate in United America is more pleasantly situated than this." Because Mount Vernon has been so carefully preserved and restored, present-day visitors to the home of the first President can see his stately mansion in the same beautiful setting that gave him so much enjoyment.


## The Museum

THE MOUNT VERNON MUSEUM, in the north lane, was built in 1928 on the site of some former slave quarters. It houses a valuable collection of books, documents, pictures, and other objects connected with the Washington family. One of the items on display is the famous bust of George Washington which was modeled at Mount Vernon in 1785 by the French sculptor Jean Antoine Houdon, who had been commissioned to do a statue of Washington by the state of Virginia. With three assistants, the sculptor traveled to Mount Vernon where he made the bust of local clay. He then took plaster impressions of it and completed the statue after returning to Paris. The original clay bust, which remained at Mount Vernon, is considered one of the best ever done of Washington.

Also on display are some of the first President's military swords and sashes, and the family Bible in which his birth is recorded. Special cases hold silver that belonged to the Washington and

Typical of the items in the museum annex is this model of Mount Vernon in an archeology and restoration exhibit. The various pieces are colored to show how the house was enlarged over the years.

Left: The Houdon bust of George Washington is now the most valuable object at Mount Vernon. Right: Clothing, household equipment and other items that belonged to George and Martha Washington are displayed in the Mount Vernon Museum.

Custis families. Martha Washington had five different sets of china, and representative pieces from each set are on display, as are several samples of her needlework.

The Mount Vernon Ladies' Association continues to add to its collection of items from Mount Vernon's illustrious past as they are located and found to be authentic. From time to time new acquisitions are displayed in the museum and there are special exhibits in a wing of the greenhouse.

*The Mount Vernon cornerstone now in the museum was removed from a cellar wall. The L W indicates that it was placed in the wall by George Washington's grandfather Lawrence, or by his half-brother Lawrence.*

*Washington's tomb.*

## Washington's Tomb

WHEN GEORGE WASHINGTON's half-brother Lawrence died at Mount Vernon in 1752, he was buried in the family tomb on a slope overlooking the Potomac River. Forty-seven years later, on Wednesday, December 18, 1799, military officers and Masons carried the body of the first President to the same vault. A naval schooner anchored in the river off Mount Vernon fired its guns at one-minute intervals, as the funeral cortege moved from the mansion house to the tomb. In the sad procession marched mounted and foot soldiers, bandsmen playing a funeral dirge on muffled drums, members of the clergy, and Washington's horse carrying an empty saddle.

Martha Washington was buried in the family tomb in 1802, and the next owner of Mount Vernon, Bushrod Washington, in 1829.

Although George Washington left specific instructions in his will that a new brick tomb was to be built, the project did not get under way for several years. In the meantime, Congress made several efforts to have the body of the first President reburied in the city of Washington, where a special crypt was prepared in the Capitol. The state of Virginia wanted to have Washington's body moved to Richmond, its capital city.

*The old Washington family tomb located on a bluff overlooking the Potomac River has been restored, but is now empty.*

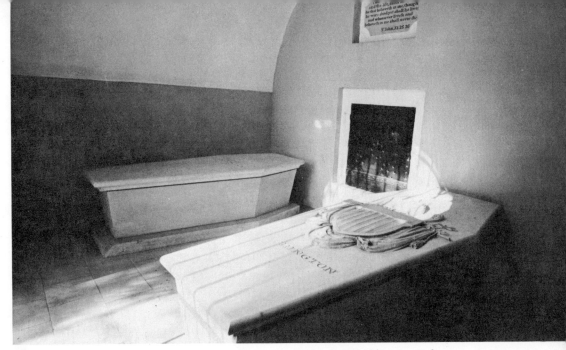

*The outer vault contains the sarcophagi of George and Martha Washington. Relatives were buried in the inner vault, the last one in 1855.*

After the death of Judge Bushrod Washington, his heir, John Augustine Washington, Sr., took over the management of Mount Vernon. In 1830, he discharged an employee who returned one night and broke into the family tomb planning to steal the skull of George Washington. The employee made off with the skull of one of Washington's nephews instead. The thief was caught, but the incident convinced the owner of Mount Vernon that a more secure tomb was needed. He arranged to have one built and, in 1831, the bodies in the old family tomb were placed in the new vault.

In 1837, an open outer vault was added to hold the two simple marble sarcophagi in which George and Martha Washington now lie buried. One is inscribed "Washington" and the other "Martha, Consort of Washington." A stone tablet above the entrance to the vault carries the inscription: "Within this Enclosure Rest the remains of Gen. George Washington."

57

## The Traditional Salute

SHIPS OF THE United States Navy pay a special tribute to the first President as they travel up and down the Potomac River. When a Navy ship passes Washington's tomb, she lowers her flag to half-mast and tolls her bell as the crew lines up at attention facing Mount Vernon, and renders a hand salute to the "Father of his Country."

The custom had its beginning during the War of 1812 when the British ship *Seahorse* tolled her bell as she passed Mount Vernon. The *Seahorse* was sailing down the Potomac River after taking part in an attack on the city of Washington. It is not known if the British, who were at war with the United States, tolled their bell as a gesture of respect or defiance, but the custom has persisted to this day.

## Washington's Grist Mill

IN COLONIAL TIMES every large estate had its own grist mill for grinding grain into flour. The mills were always located on streams because water supplied the power for turning the heavy millstones that crushed the grain.

George Washington's father built Mount Vernon's grist mill on Dogue Run some time between 1735 and 1739. In addition to a stone millhouse, there was a house for the miller, and a shop for the cooper who made and repaired the barrels that held the grain.

After George Washington became the owner of Mount Vernon, he took a great interest in the operation of the mill and visited it almost every day when he was at home. In 1770, he rebuilt the mill and, in 1795, he repaired the millrace that carried water to the mill wheel.

*Members of the Third Infantry Regiment's Honor Guard Company, dressed in colonial uniforms, add a colorful touch to ceremonial occasions at Mount Vernon. This picture was taken at the west front of the mansion.*

The Mount Vernon mill operated for many years after George Washington's death, but eventually it was abandoned and its stones were used for other buildings. When the Virginia Conservation Commission acquired the site of the mill in 1932, only the foundation remained. Using Washington's letters and diaries and other Mount Vernon records as a guide, the Commission located another old mill very similar to the one that once operated on Dogue Run.

*Washington's Grist Mill with the miller's white clapboard cottage in the background.*

That mill was disassembled and rebuilt on the foundation of Washington's mill. The miller's white clapboard cottage was also rebuilt. Washington's two mill ponds were no longer in existence, but the millrace and the water gates were restored.

As a result of the efforts of the Commission, visitors to the mill, located approximately three miles from the Mount Vernon mansion house, can see the same kind of wheels, grinding stones, boxes for sifting grain, and "cooper's horses" for bending barrel staves and hoops that George Washington saw on his frequent visits to the mill.

## Woodlawn Plantation

ON FEBRUARY 22, 1799, George Washington wrote in his diary: "Miss Custis was married abt. Candle light to Mr. Lawe. Lewis." He was recording the wedding of Eleanor (Nelly) Parke Custis, Martha Washington's granddaughter and his adopted daughter, to Lawrence Lewis, the son of Betty Washington Lewis, the General's only sister. Lawrence, a favorite nephew, acted as secretary and deputy host for his uncle after he came to live at Mount Vernon in the summer of 1797.

Washington was genuinely fond of both young people and encouraged their marriage. As a wedding gift, he set aside two thousand acres of his Mount Vernon estate, which they were to inherit after his death. It included part of his Dogue Run Farm, his grist mill, and his distillery. He recommended a big hill on the property as "a most beautiful site for a Gentleman's Seat." This was where the Lewises built the house which they called Woodlawn.

Woodlawn, designed by Dr. William Thornton, a friend of Washington and the architect of the National Capitol, was completed in 1805. Like Mount Vernon, it is Georgian in style and famous for its architectural beauty. The house is surrounded by

*Woodlawn.*

extensive grounds and gardens, and has a fine view of the Potomac River.

Woodlawn's first floor is divided into a central hall and four principal rooms — a dining room and a music room on one side and a parlor and a bedroom on the other. There are four bedrooms on the second floor. Nelly Lewis brought some of the furniture now in the rooms at Woodlawn from Mount Vernon when she moved into her new home.

The Lewises entertained many famous guests while they lived at Woodlawn. The Marquis de Lafayette stayed there during his trip to America in 1824. Zachary Taylor, Andrew Jackson, Millard Fillmore, and Henry Clay all visited at Woodlawn.

Nelly Lewis lived at Woodlawn until 1839. Several years later her heirs sold the estate. Until 1948, no attempt was made to preserve the historic house which had deteriorated over the years. Then a group of public-spirited citizens acquired the property and began to restore it. Today, Woodlawn is considered one of the most interesting of America's historic houses. It is open to the public and administered by the National Trust for Historical Preservation.

## Pohick Church

MOST OF THE early settlers in Virginia were members of the Church of England. In their new home they organized parishes and built churches similar to the ones they had left behind in England. The residents of the area around Mount Vernon organized Truro Parish in 1732.

George Washington's father was a vestryman of Truro Parish while he lived at Mount Vernon. In those days a vestryman was responsible for the care of the poor, and the morals of the community in general. George Washington served as a vestryman of Truro from 1762 until 1784. While he was a vestryman, Pohick Church, the principal church of Truro Parish, was built to replace an earlier structure. Pohick received its name from a stream in the vicinity.

Washington and the other large landowners of the parish took an active interest in the construction of the new church. Using his experience as a surveyor, Washington is said to have drawn an elaborate map to prove that the new church should be located two miles closer to Mount Vernon than the old one. He is also credited with working out the ground plan for Pohick Church.

After Pohick Church was completed in 1772, George Washington attended many services there. Mason L. Weems, a biographer

*Pohick Church and some of its ancient grave markers.*

of Washington and the man responsible for many stories of Washington's youth (including the mythical incident of George confessing that he had chopped down his father's cherry tree), was a rector at Pohick.

The church fell into disuse in the years after the Revolutionary War, but, in 1840, it underwent extensive renovation. During the Civil War, Union troops stationed in the area disfigured the outside of the building and destroyed most of the interior. They moved the ancient baptismal font out of the church and used it to water their horses.

Another restoration of Pohick Church began late in the nineteenth century. The original baptismal font was located on a neighboring farm and returned to the church, but the rest of the furnishings are reproductions.

Today, Pohick Church, which is still lighted by candles, has an active Episcopal congregation.

# A Mount Vernon Chronology

1674   John Washington and Nicholas Spencer receive a grant of 5,000 acres of land on the Potomac River.

1690   The Washingtons and Spencers divide their property. The Washington half is called Little Hunting Creek Plantation.

1726   Augustine Washington, George Washington's father, becomes the owner of Little Hunting Creek Plantation.

1735   Augustine Washington moves his family to Little Hunting Creek Plantation.

1735-39   George Washington spends four boyhood years at Little Hunting Creek Plantation.

1739   Augustine Washington moves his family to Fredericksburg, Virginia.

1740   Augustine Washington gives Little Hunting Creek Plantation to his son Lawrence.

1743   Augustine Washington dies. Lawrence changes the name of Little Hunting Creek Plantation to Mount Vernon and settles there with his bride.

1743-52   George Washington spends much of his time at Mount Vernon.

1752   Lawrence Washington dies and is buried at Mount Vernon.

1754    George Washington becomes the owner of Mount Vernon.

1754-59    Military service in the French and Indian War keeps Washington away from Mount Vernon. His house is enlarged and remodeled during his absence.

1759    Washington marries Martha Custis and brings her and her two young children to Mount Vernon.

1759-75    George Washington lives at Mount Vernon. He enlarges his house and develops his plantation.

1775    Chosen to command the Continental Army in the Revolutionary War, Washington leaves Mount Vernon and is away for the next eight years. His cousin Lund Washington manages the estate.

1783    Washington resigns his commission as Commander in Chief of the Continental Army and returns to Mount Vernon.

1789-97    Elected the first President of the United States, Washington lives first in New York and then in Philadelphia. He visits Mount Vernon only occasionally.

1797    Washington declines a third Presidential term and retires to Mount Vernon.

1797-99    Washington takes an active part in the management of his estate.

1799    Nelly Custis and Lawrence Lewis are married at Mount Vernon on February 22.

1799   George Washington dies on December 14, and is buried in the family tomb.

1802   Martha Washington dies and Bushrod Washington inherits 4,000 acres of the Mount Vernon estate.

1829   Bushrod Washington dies and leaves Mount Vernon to John Augustine Washington, Sr.

1831   A new Washington family tomb replaces the old burial vault.

1850   John Augustine Washington, Jr., becomes the last private owner of Mount Vernon.

1853   Miss Ann Pamela Cunningham begins her drive to save Mount Vernon.

1858   The Mount Vernon Ladies' Association receives a charter from the state of Virginia and purchases the Mount Vernon mansion house and 200 acres of the estate from John Augustine Washington, Jr.

1859   The Association begins the restoration of Mount Vernon.

## General Information

*Mount Vernon*

    Visiting hours: 9 A.M. to 5 P.M. from March 1 to September 30
                       9 A.M. to 4 P.M. from October 1 to February 28
    Admission fee: Adults — 75¢
                    Children — free
    Route from Washington, D. C.: South on Mount Vernon National Highway (16 miles).

*Washington's Grist Mill*

    Visiting hours: Daylight hours during the tourist season.
    Admission fee: Adults — 25¢
                    Children — 10¢
    Route from Washington, D. C.: South on Mount Vernon National Highway and Virginia 235 (18 miles).

*Woodlawn Plantation*

    Visiting hours: 9:30 A.M. to 4:30 P.M.
    Admission fee: Adults — 75¢
                    Children — 35¢
    Route from Washington, D. C.: South on Route 1 (13 miles).

*Pohick Church*

    Visiting hours: 9 A.M. to 5 P.M. daily.
    Admission fee: Free; donations are welcome.
    Route from Washington, D. C.: South on Route 1 (15 miles).

# Index

Bassett, Fanny, 16
Blueskin (GW's horse), 42
*Bonhomme Richard*, 18
Braddock, General, 6

Chippendale furnishings, 20
Church of England, 63
Civil War, 64
Clay, Henry, 62
Congress, U.S., 56
Continental Congress, 7
Craik, Dr. James, 23, 26
Cunningham, Ann Pamela, 8, 67
Custis, George Washington Parke, 21, 26, 30
Custis, Martha Parke, 27

Dogue Run, 58, 60
    Farm, 61

Fairfax, Lord Thomas, 40
Fairfax, William, 6
Fillmore, Millard, 62
French and Indian War, 6, 66
French Revolution, 12

Gregory, Mildred Washington, 3
Grist Mill. *See* Washington's Grist Mill.

Houdon, Jean Antoine, 52

Jackson, Andrew, 62
Jones, John Paul, 18

Lafayette, George Washington, 16
Lafayette, Marquis de, 12, 16, 30, 62
Lewis, Betty Washington (GW's sister), 61
Lewis, Lawrence (GW's nephew), 18, 61, 67

Lewis, Nelly Custis, 17-18, 21, 27, 30, 61, 62, 63, 67
Little Hunting Creek Plantation, 3, 65

Magnolia (racehorse), 42
Mansion House Farm, 2, 46
Maryland, 52
Mount Vernon (estate):
    activities done on, 37-43, 46-47
    bowling green, 50, 52
    coach house, 40, 44
    gardener's house, 46
    gardens, 2, 47, 49, 50
    greenhouse, 47, 50, 54
    restoration, 1, 8-9, 18
    size, 2
    smokehouse, 40
    spinning house, 46
    stable, 42-43, 44
    storehouse, 46
    washhouse, 40
    Washington's improvements on, 6-8
    *See also* Mount Vernon Museum, Washington's tomb, Washington's Grist Mill, and Woodlawn Plantation.
Mount Vernon Ladies' Association of the Union, 1, 8-9, 24, 44, 47-48, 54, 67
    *See also* Mount Vernon: restoration.
Mount Vernon Mansion House:
    architecture, 9
    banquet hall, 12, 22
    bedrooms, 21-22, 26-31, 32
    Blue Bedroom, 28-30
    butler's house, 37-40
    dining schedule, 36
    family dining room, 20-21
    first floor, 11-26

kitchen, 25, 33-37
Lafayette Room, 31
library, 22-23, 24, 26
little parlor, 17-18
music room, 17
Nelly Custis Room, 31
pantry, 25-26
"the passage," 11
piazza, 9-10, 11
second floor, 26-31
third floor, 32
the Washingtons' quarters, 26-28
west parlor, 15-16
Yellow Bedroom, 31
*See also* Mount Vernon (estate), Mount Vernon Mansion House Farm, Little Hunting Creek Plantation, and Mount Vernon Museum.
Mount Vernon Museum, 52-54

National Trust for Historical Preservation, 63
Navy, U.S., 58
Nelson (GW's horse), 42
Nelson, General Thomas, 42
New York, 7, 66

Peale, Charles Wilson, 16
Philadelphia, 7, 66
Pine, Robert Edge, 16, 27
Pohick Church, 63-64
Potomac River, 10, 31, 52, 55, 58, 62, 65

Revolutionary War, 6, 7, 12, 18, 23, 27, 28, 42, 64, 66, 67
Richmond (Virginia), 56

*Seahorse*, 58
*Serapis*, 18
Sharples, James, 16
Slave quarters, 51
Spencer, Nicholas, 3, 7, 65

Taylor, Zachary, 62

Thornton, Dr. William, 61
Truro Parish, 63-64
*See also* Pohick Church.

Vaughan, Samuel, 14-15
Vernon, Edward, 3
Virginia, 1, 3, 5, 6, 15, 26, 50, 56, 63
Virginia Conservation Commission, 60-61

Wakefield estate, 3
War of 1812, 58
Washington, Augustine (GW's father), 3, 63, 65
Washington, Bushrod (GW's nephew), 8, 24, 56, 57, 67
Washington, George, 1-8, 9, 11, 12, 14, 15, 16, 17, 18, 20-24, 26, 27, 28, 31, 32, 49-52, 55-57, 58, 63-64, 65, 66, 67
coat of arms, 15, 16-17
Washington, John (GW's brother), 6
Washington, John (GW's great-grandfather), 3
Washington, John Augustine, Sr. (GW's grandnephew), 8, 57, 67
Washington, John Augustine, Jr. (GW's great-grandnephew), 8, 67
Washington, Lawrence (GW's brother), 3-5, 55
Washington, Lawrence (GW's grandfather), 3, 65
Washington, Lund (GW's cousin), 7, 12, 21, 66
Washington, Martha Dandridge Custis, 1, 6, 16, 20, 21, 25, 26, 27, 28, 31, 32, 54, 56, 57, 61, 66, 67
Washington, Sarah, 5
Washington, D.C., 56
Washington's Grist Mill, 58-61
Washington's tomb, 55-57
traditional salute at, 58
Weems, Mason L. ("Parson Weems"), 63-64
Woodlawn Plantation, 18, 61-63
architecture, 61
furnishings, 62